Eh Canada?

Eh Canada?

Wit and Wisdom from the Frozen North

Selected and Introduced by
Eliakim Katz

Published in 1999 by Stoddart Publishing Co. Limited
34 Lesmill Road, Toronto, Canada M3B 2T6

Distributed in Canada by General Distribution Services Limited
325 Humber College Blvd., Toronto, Ontario M9W 7C3
Tel. (416) 213-1919   Fax (416) 213-1917
Email Customer.Service@ccmailgw.genpub.com

Distributed in the U.S. by General Distribution Services Inc.
85 River Rock Drive, Suite 202, Buffalo, New York 14207
Toll-free tel. 1-800-805-1083 Toll-free fax 1-800-481-6207
Email gdsinc@genpub.com

03 02 01 00 99 1 2 3 4 5

Cataloguing in Publication Data

Katz, Eliakim
Eh Canada?: wit and wisdom from the frozen North

ISBN 0-7737-6030-X

1. Canadians — Humor.   2. Canada — Humor.   3. Canadians — Quotations.
4. Canada — Quotations, maxims, etc.   5. Canadian wit and humor (English).*
6. Quotations, English. I. Katz, Eliakim.

PN6178.C3E3   1999   971'.002'07   C99-931453-X

Cover design: Angel Guerra
Design and typesetting: Kinetics Design & Illustration

Canad^ä

THE CANADA COUNCIL | LE CONSEIL DES ARTS
FOR THE ARTS | DU CANADA
SINCE 1957 | DEPUIS 1957

We acknowledge for their financial support of our publishing program the Canada Council, the Ontario Arts Council, and the Government of Canada through the Book Publishing Industry Development Program (BPIDP).

Printed and bound in Canada

To my children

— Akiva, Tamara, Lia, and Keren —

who are already much more Canadian

than I'll ever be

Acknowledgments

I wish to thank my children for helping me research this book. In addition, I want to thank Jim Gifford, my editor at Stoddart, for his patient and painstaking support. On a less practical but more profound level I also want to thank the many individuals whose reflections on the Canadian experience constitute this book.

Introduction

$\mathcal{A}$ few weeks after the end of the Gulf War, my parents-in-law, who live in Israel, came to visit us in Toronto. They flew in via New York. All six of us awaited them at the airport.

They were not the first to emerge. Nor the second.

We waited as the stream of passengers from their flight decreased to a trickle, and then ceased altogether. The was no sign of my in-laws. The kids showed symptoms of impatience. The younger generation does not find landings and takeoffs quite as exciting as I used to.

Then, two and a half hours after their flight had landed, my bewildered in-laws finally emerged. Our applause was tumultuous.

"What happened? Was anything wrong?" we asked.

"No," they said. "Not wrong, but a little bit strange."

Upon seeing their Israeli passports, the immigration officer had sent them for a second interview.

"Nothing personal," he assured them cheerfully, explaining that all travellers from the Middle East had to be screened carefully. Standing orders.

"But why?" they asked.

The immigration official looked down. "Terrorism, you know," he mumbled.

"But both of us are over seventy," my father-in-law protested. "Our days of terrorism are over."

"Yes," said the official, refusing to meet their eyes. "But as a government agency we do not practise age-discrimination."

In many ways my in-laws' experience captures the essence of Canada. The Woody Allen of nations, it is full of good intentions, etc.

Try this: Close your eyes and think of Canada. It's guaranteed not to hurt.

Canada may not hurt, but it doesn't excite either. Canada does not conjure images of money, or sex, or war, or passion. Thinking of Canada does not quicken your pulse. Adrenaline will not rush into your blood stream. Your blood pressure will not shoot up.

When you think of Canada, you think of lakes, of vast expanses of snowy prairies, of eternal forests. Canada has been described as "the retarded giant on your doorstep." I beg to differ. Canada is an

above average (though not outstanding) gentle giant, who very often feels dwarfed by other nations.

Canada is a national experiment in the Garden of Eden. Safe but boring, it treads the thin line between contentment and ennui. It is Clark Kent rather than Superman or Lex Luther.

Canada is reality. Not as rich or powerful as some, not as poor as others, the struggles of Canada parallel those of most of us. Nothing heroic, nothing dangerous, just the details of everyday life against the background of bouts of existential angst.

Canada is obsessed with its identity, with its sense of inferiority and with its separation anxiety. It is forever comparing, but only with the best.

However, despite rumours to the contrary, Canadians can and do laugh at themselves. Often. Of course, non-Canadians also laugh at Canada, though a little less frequently. In many ways, Canada is a private joke.

This book attempts to make public and humorous some of the pains and pleasures of Canada as reflected in the words of Canadians and non-Canadians. If you had thought that Canada is not funny, this book may change your mind.

O Canada! We don't know what you are.
Nation, we thought, but that Quebec doth bar.
And a colony you had ceased to be,
So we know what you are not;
And we stand on guard,
Though it's rather hard,
When we're not quite sure for what.
O Canada! Great Undefined!
O Canada! Can't you make up your mind?
O Canada! Can't you some status find?

— *Eugene Forsey*

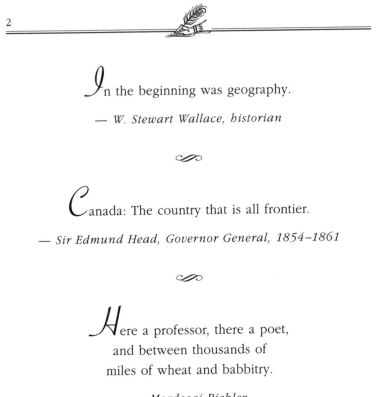

*I*n the beginning was geography.

— *W. Stewart Wallace, historian*

*C*anada: The country that is all frontier.

— *Sir Edmund Head, Governor General, 1854–1861*

*H*ere a professor, there a poet,
and between thousands of
miles of wheat and babbitry.

— *Mordecai Richler*

*T*he Canadian is mildewed with caution.

— *Marshall McLuhan*

*Y*ou have to know a man awfully well in Canada
to know his surname.

— *Lord Tweedsmuir*

*T*he land too poor for any other crop,
it is best for raising men.

— *Roger Pocock,*
Canadian pioneer, c. 1900

*W*e are not a special people
nor are we a Chosen People.
We live in a Chosen Land.

— *Ralph Allen, Canadian journalist*

*I*f some countries have too much history,
we have too much geography.

— *William Lyon Mackenzie King, Prime Minister*

*C*anada needs only to be known to be great.

— *J. Castel Hopkins, 1901*

$\mathcal{W}$e live in an empty place filled with wonders.

— *Peter C. Newman*

$\backsim$

$\mathcal{C}$anada is like an expanding flower —
wherever you look you see some fresh petal unrolling.

— *Sir Arthur Conan Doyle*

$\backsim$

$\mathcal{T}$he country, so wild and grand,
is of itself enough to interest anyone
in its wonderful dreariness.

— *John James Audubon, 1833*

*I*t is a peculiar Canadian trait to be
able to spot an inequity better at a distance,
especially if facing south, than close up.

— *George Bain*

*O*ur national soul has not grown beyond infancy.

— *Marius Barbeau*

*C*anada's neuroses range from an
inferiority complex to separation anxiety.

— *Elliott Priest*

*I*f the national mental illness of the United States is megalomania, that of Canada is paranoid schizophrenia.

— *Margaret Atwood*

A Canadian is an unarmed American with a health plan.

— *Brad Green*

*O*n our Canadian climate I've little to say,
As I've lived in it many years and cold day,
This present month, October, without strife,
Is the Beautifullest I ever saw in my life.

— *James Gay, 1885*

*T*he prettiest Sunday afternoon drive in the world.

— *Winston Churchill, on the Niagara Parkway, 1943*

*G*reat thoughts or deeds are not bred by scenery.

— *John G. Bourinot, 1893*

*N*ot until I came to Canada
did I realize that snow was a four-letter word.

— *Alberto Manguel, Argentine-born Canadian author*

*I*n land so bleak and bare
A single plume of smoke
is a scroll of history.

— *F.R. Scott, poet*

[*T*] his is a country
where a man can die

                simply from being

caught outside

— *Alden Nowlan, poet*

*T*his is the law of the Yukon, that
    only the strong shall thrive;
That surely the weak shall perish,
    and only the fit survive.
Dissolute, damned and despairful,
    crippled and palsied and slain,
This is the will of the Yukon —
    Lo, how she makes it plain!

— *Robert W. Service*

*Y*ou don't own the land. In winter, the elements own it,
and in summer, the mosquitoes.

— *Don Currie*

*H*udson Bay is certainly a country that Sinbad the Sailor
never saw, as he never makes mention of mosquitoes.

— *David Thompson, 1784*

I fear that I have not got much to say about Canada,
not having seen much;
what I got by going to Canada was a cold.

— *Henry David Thoreau, 1850*

$\mathcal{C}$anada is not a country for the cold of heart or the cold of feet.

— *Pierre Trudeau*

$\mathcal{O}$h, it's 40 below in the winter,
And it's 20 below in the fall.
It rises to zero in springtime,
And we ain't got no summer, at all.

— *Anonymous*

$\mathcal{M}$y country's not a country, it's winter.

— *Gilles Vigneault*

There was a small boy of Quebec
Who was buried in snow to his neck
When they said "Are you Friz?"
He replied "Yes, I is —
But we don't call this cold in Quebec."

— *Rudyard Kipling*

I am proud to be an Eskimo but I think that we can improve on the igloo as a permanent dwelling.

— *Abraham Okpik, Inuit spokesperson*

*I*n the past, people went North for gold, God or Glory. Now, no one steps over the 60th parallel without claiming he is going to help the native people.

— *Jim Lotz*

*C*anadian history is to be found where there has been no Canadian history, in the North.

— *W.L. Morton, Canadian historian*

*W*hen the white man came we had the land
and they had the Bibles; now they have the land
and we have the Bibles.

— *Chief Dan George*

*I*nuit have many words for snow but no word for camel.

— *John MacDonald, government official*

*T*here are too many Eskimos and not enough seals.

— *Imre Madách, 1861*

*I*n Canada there is too much of everything.
Too much rock,
Too much prairie,
Too much tundra,
Too much mountain,
Too much forest.
Above all, too much forest.

— *Edward McCourt*

*E*conomically,
Canada is not yet out of the woods.

— *Elliott Priest*

$\mathcal{Y}$ou will make a better job sawing wood if you
know Euclid than if you don't.

— *William Pendergast, 1890s*

∞

$\mathcal{T}$here is nothing disgraceful about being hewers of wood
and drawers of water if that is where you find your
competitive advantage.

— *James Gillies*

*A*ny Canadian can look outward to almost infinity,
and call it his own.

— *Roderick Haig-Brown*

*T*o enter the United States is a matter of crossing the ocean;
to enter Canada is a matter of being silently swallowed
by an alien continent.

— *Northrop Frye*

*C*anada [is] the most substantial of countries,
where nothing seems to end.

— *Jan Morris*

*P*ublish or Prairies!

— Anonymous admonition to aspiring academics

*E*dmonton isn't really the end of the world — although
you can see it from there.

— Ralph Klein

*W*hen they said Canada,
I thought it would be up in
the mountains somewhere.

— *Marilyn Monroe*

*C*anada is so far away it hardly exists.

— *Jorge Luis Borges*

I don't even know what street Canada is on.

— *Al Capone*

*G*iven any form of incursion by foreign troops into the
Canadian Arctic — provided we ever found out
about it — we could do nothing except send
a Mountie in a skidoo to give out parking tickets.

— *Peter C. Newman*

*W*e are guarded by Generals Atlantic and Pacific.

— *F.H. Underhill and F.R. Scott*

*A*ny Canadian proposal for disarmament is,
in the end, a proposal that someone else disarm.

— *E.L.M. Burns, Canadian general*

$\mathcal{Y}$ou've probably heard that we can ski within sight
of downtown Vancouver and be on the water catching
a spring salmon, all in the space of thirty minutes.
It's true — as long as your skis have quick-release bindings.
Otherwise, it might take up to forty-five minutes.

— *Denny Boyd*

$\mathcal{B}$ritish Columbia is a large body of land
entirely surrounded by envy.

— *Eric Nicol*

$\mathcal{V}$ancouver is less than meets the eye.

— *William Thorsell, journalist*

$\mathcal{V}$ancouver is the suicide capital of the country.
You keep going west until you run out. You come to the edge.
Then you fall off.

— *Margaret Atwood*

$\mathcal{L}$ife must be swell in a province where,
when they are hungry, all they have to do is
go into the garden and eat roses.

— *Cynthia Berney Wine, food specialist, on BC*

$\mathcal{V}$ictoria is 3,000 miles from Ottawa whereas
Ottawa is 30,000 miles from Victoria.

— *Edward G. Prior, BC Premier*

*E*dmonton, like acne, is to be endured.

— *Mordecai Richler*

*E*dmonton:
Exciting, perhaps even colourful, but tough,
a city I would not like to be unemployed in.

— *Alistair Horne*

*W*hy should I want to run Canada when
I already run Alberta?

— *Peter Lougheed*

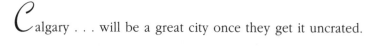

*C*algary . . . will be a great city once they get it uncrated.

— *Allan Fotheringham*

*C*algary is surely the only major North American city where, as a reflection of its cow-town past, auto expressways are still called trails.

— *John M. Scott*

*S*askatchewan is much like Texas — except it's more
friendly to the United States.

— *Adlai Stevenson*

I met the Mafia; when I told them I had worked for the
Saskatchewan government, they were very much impressed.

— *Graham Spry, Agent-General for Saskatchewan in the UK*

*S*askatchewan, the land of snow,
Where winds are always on the blow,
Where people sit with frozen toes,
And why we stay here no one knows.

— *Canadian folksong*

*T*he Lord said "let there be wheat"
and Saskatchewan was born.

— *Stephen Leacock*

*N*o one is born in the prairies who can help it,
and no one dies there who can get out in time.

— *Anonymous*

If You're So Good, What Are You Doing in Saskatoon?

— *title of a popular Prairie drama, early 1980s*

No cities with the possible exception of Sodom and Gomorra have ever been founded in less congenial physical surroundings than Regina, Queen of Saskatchewan.

— *Edward McCourt, writer*

I am rather inclined to believe that this is the land that God gave to Cain.

— *Jacques Cartier*

*W*innipeg is a hundred dollars from anywhere.

— *Anonymous, about 1900*

*C*ommitting suicide in Winnipeg is redundant.

— *Anonymous*

The climate of Manitoba consists of seven months of Arctic weather and five months of cold weather.

— *Anonymous*

Geographically, Winnipeg is in the wrong place.

— *Kenneth Thomson*

"*Boy* meets girl in Winnipeg and Who Cares?"

— *title of essay by Hugh MacLennan*

*T*oronto is a kind of New York operated by the Swiss.

— *Peter Ustinov*

*T*oronto is the city of the future — and always will be.

— *Allan Lamport*

"*V*andalism hits Toronto the good" — they'd found
a scratch on one of the subway seat covers.

— *Eric Korn*

*M*y centennial project is to try to love Toronto.

— *Robert Stanfield, 1967*

*M*alicious, grudging, vindictive, implacable.

— *Margaret Atwood, on Toronto*

I was born in "Toronto the Good,"
and as it became less good it got better.

— *Sam Sniderman, "Sam the Record Man"*

*S*ome people achieve happiness,
and some just live in Toronto.

— *Emily G. Murphy, pioneer and writer*

*O*ntario has a third of the population
and half of everything else.

— *Anonymous*

*G*ive us a place to stand
And a place to grow
And call this place
Ontario.

— *Richard Morris*

*Y*ou can walk on any street in Ottawa at any time
of night and be safe. However, you could be lonely.

— *Dalton Camp*

*O*ttawa is a sub-arctic village converted by
royal mandate into a political cockpit.

— *Goldwin Smith*

*R*emember, you are not living in sin.
You are living in Ottawa. Sin is across the river.

— *Anonymous*

*O*ttawa is a strange city. You can't love it as you do Montreal, but you can't hate it as you do Toronto.

— *Ronald Lee*

✑

*T*he best thing about Ottawa
is the train to Montreal.

— *Jean Marchand*

*M*ontreal is only a stop on the way
from Belgium to Kentucky.

— *Jacques Ferron*

*I*t is the destiny of Montreal to show the country
from time to time what poetry is.

— *Louis Dudek*

*M*ontreal has become a city where you awaken
to count your losses.

— *Mordecai Richler*

*M*ontreal is the only place where a good
French accent isn't a social asset.

— *Brendan Behan*

*T*his is the first time I was ever
in a city where you couldn't throw a brick
without breaking a church window.

— *Mark Twain on Montreal*

*Q*uebec is a part of Canada in much
the same way as a cat in the mouth of
a crocodile is part of the crocodile.

— *Yves Beauchemin*

I'm a Quebecker. I was born alienated.

— *Laurier LaPierre*

*Q*uebec is a province with the longest
undefended border in Canada.

— *Dalton Camp*

*T*he Inuit have many words for white.
The Québécois have many words for discontent.

— *Elliott Priest*

*Q*uebec is one of the ten provinces
against which Canada is defending itself.

— *Carl Dubuc*

My father spoke French with a Bank of Montreal accent.

— *Hartland de Montarville Molson*

It is better to be sincere in one language
than to be a twit in two.

— *John Crosbie*

When Canadians are asked the difference
between their country and the United States,
they should answer in French.

— *Lester B. Pearson*

*M*y own Plains of Abraham,
this is what I experience when
I must speak English on a bus.

— *Paul Villeneuve*

*W*e want to speak French
and eat three meals a day.

— *Ron LaSalle*

From the day a Nova Scotian is born until the day he dies,
he knows he is right.

— *Dorothy Duncan*

The Nova Scotian . . . is the gentleman known throughout
America as Mr. Blue Nose, a sobriquet acquired from
a superior potato of that name.

— *Thomas C. Haliburton*

If Edison had lived in Nova Scotia, you might be
reading this by candlelight.

— *Tom Gray*

[*T*]he people of PEI] were quite under the impression that the Dominion has been annexed to Prince Edward.

— *Lord Dufferin*

I was selected to run New Brunswick. No one said I had to live there.

— *Richard Hatfield*

*C*anada is like an old cow. The West feeds it. Ontario and Quebec milk it. And you can imagine what it's doing in the Maritimes.

— *T.C. Douglas*

*T*here is an end to most things,
even to a Newfoundland storm.

— *Sir John Alcock*

*T*he purity of the air in Newfoundland
is without doubt due to the fact that the people of
the outports never open their windows.

— *J.G. Millais, 1907*

*M*ost Newfoundlanders believe that trying to understand
Canadians has been found to cause tumours in rats.

— *Ray Guy*

*I*n Cod we trust.

— *graffiti, Newfoundland, 1963*

*N*othing fishy here.

— *graffiti, Newfoundland, 1996*

*I*t might be said that we all live in one big house.
Welcome to the attic.

— *Gordon Pinsent, welcoming Ronald Reagan to Canada*

*C*anada and Mexico, as the saying goes,
have one common problem between them.

— *J.C.M. Ogelsby*

*O*ne thing Canada has never been to Americans
is understood.

— *Andrew H. Malcolm*

Canada's role is to interpret the real meaning
of the US to the rest of the world.

— *Marshall McLuhan*

The Americans are our best friends,
whether we like it or not.

— *Robert Thompson, politician*

Although nearly all Canadian holidays are the same as
American ones, Canadian Thanksgiving is held a month early
since Canadians don't have so much to be thankful for.

— *Jack McIver*

*T*he main business of Canadian foreign relations
is to remain friendly with the United States while
preserving its own self-respect.

— *Sir Clifford Sifton*

*T*he only way to get away from the influence of
the American economy would be to float our half of the
continent off somewhere else.

— *John Kenneth Galbraith*

*C*anada is a very nice place.
And we intend to keep it that way.

— *J.P. Morgan*

*T*he advantage of living in Canada, in general,
is to watch the United States making fools of themselves.

— *Marshall McLuhan*

*L*iving next to [the United States] is in some ways
like sleeping with an elephant.
No matter how friendly and even-tempered the beast,
one is affected by every twitch and grunt.

— *Pierre Trudeau*

*W*hy don't we give the country to the Americans?
They seem to want it so much more than we do.

— *Dian Cohen*

*S*ome sixty years ago Sir Wilfrid Laurier declared
that the twentieth century belongs to Canada.
By the middle of the century it had become clear
that Canada belongs to the United States.

— *Kari Levitt*

*C*anadian nationality being a lost cause,
the ultimate union of Canada with the United States
appears now to be morally certain.

— *Goldwin Smith, 1878*

*T*here are parts of Canada still owned by the Canadians,
but they are too scattered to make a country.

— *Louis Dudek*

∞

*O*urs is a sovereign nation
Bows to no foreign will
But whenever they cough in Washington
They spit in Parliament Hill.

— *Joe Wallace*

*C*anadians don't export.
We permit others to import from us.

— *Jean-Luc Pepin*

❧

*I*f Canada invented the wheel, it would drag
it on a sled to be marketed in the United States.

— *Denzil Doyle*

❧

*C*anada in a non-conductor of any sort
of intellectual current.

— *Frederick Philip Grove*

*J*ohn Kenneth Galbraith and Marshall McLuhan are the two greatest modern Canadians the United States has produced.

— *Anthony Burgess*

*I*n the United States they run with the ball.
In Canada, we apply for a government grant to get the money to buy the ball.

— *Geraldine Kennedy-Wallace, Canadian scientist*

*C*anada is a live country, live,
but not like the States, kicking.

— *Rupert Brooke*

*T*he Yankees in the land abound
For Uncle Sam gets all around
And with his push and grit and go
Is sure to make the country grow

— *E.F. Miller, 1911, on Americans settling*
in the Canadian prairies

*M*y generation of Canadians grew up believing
that if we were very good or very smart, or both,
we would some day graduate from Canada.

— *Robert Fulford*

*M*oving to the United States is part of Canadian culture.

— *Desmond Morton*

*C*anada's story begins in Lamentations and ends in Exodus.

— *popular saying on PEI, around 1900*

*L*os Angeles,
with some 500,000 Canadians
who have settled here,
is Canada's fourth largest city.

— *Jack Kent Cooke*

*F*our and twenty Yankees, feeling very dry,
Went across the border to get a drink of rye.
When the rye was opened, the Yanks began to sing,
"God bless America, but God save the King!"

— *Anonymous, to the Duke of Windsor, 1919*

*W*e had to leave to be recognized. It was an anomaly.
If we stayed we were nobodies. If we went away
and were successful, we were resented.

— *Arthur Hill, Saskatchewan-born actor*

∽

*W*e also exclude rapists, drug pushers and terrorists,
not just Canadians.

— *US Immigration and Naturalization Service spokesperson*

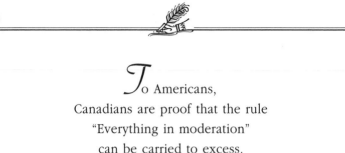

To Americans,
Canadians are proof that the rule
"Everything in moderation"
can be carried to excess.

— *Eric Nicol*

"Thank you" is excellent, but formal and English in effect.
"Thanks a million" is excellent, but it has an American
extravagance which is unbecoming in Canadian mouths.
What would you think of "Thanks a hundred thousand"?
It seems to me to strike the right Canadian note.

— *Robertson Davies*

$\mathcal{C}$anada is a permanent compromise.

— *Jan Morris*

$\mathcal{T}$he father of Confederation is deadlock.

— *Godwin Smith*

$\mathcal{W}$e are the orphans of Confederation
and we resent it.

— *Izzy Asper, on Western Canada*

*C*anadian economic history is more than
US economic history with snow on it.

— *T.H.B. Symons*

*H*appy nations, someone said, have no history —
an aphorism of possible consolation to Canadians.

— *Dalton Camp*

*C*anadians are people who remember their present
and think it's their history.

— *J. Michael Bliss*

The tragedy of this country is
that the French Canadians never forget history,
and the English Canadians never remember.

— *John Roberts*

We French, we English,
never lost our civil war,
endure it still,
a bloodless silly bore.

— *Earle Birney*

*W*henever I'm away from Canada
the thing I miss most is the apathy.

— *Mendelson Joe*

*T*he beaver is a good national symbol for Canada.
He's so busy chewing he can't see what's going on.

— *Howard Cable*

*M*uch will have to change in Canada
if the country is to stay the same.

— *Abraham Rotstein*

*T*he Canadian kid who wants to grow up to be
prime minister isn't thinking big, he's setting a limit
on his ambitions rather early.

— *Mordecai Richler*

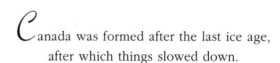

*C*anada was formed after the last ice age,
after which things slowed down.

— *Eric Nicol*

*T*ranscendental meditation, the prolonged effort to think of
nothing, is a technique perfectly suitable for Canadians.
They've been practising it for almost a century.

— *Louis Dudek*

*C*anadians are prejudiced in favour of the ordinary.

— *Charles Taylor*

*T*he traffic lights at the CBC are forever amber.

— *Fletcher Markle, CBC producer*

*W*hy did the Canadian cross the road?
To get to the middle . . .

— *Allan Fotheringham*

$\mathcal{C}$anadians are a meek bunch; they'll take orders
from anybody in uniform, including the milkman.

— *A.R.M. Lower*

$\mathcal{J}$ am a respecter of institutions.
Even in Paris I remained a Canadian.
I puffed hashish, but I didn't inhale.

— *Mordecai Richler*

[*C*anada's] inhabitants have achieved the expected impossible by contriving a boring whisky.

— *Kingsley Amis*

*O*ne of Canada's greatest tragedies is that the sober second thoughts so often prevail.

— *Richard J. Needham*

*C*anada is the only country in the world where passion is mistaken for asthma.

— *Anonymous*

[*C*anada] is not a country you love.
It's a country you worry about.

— *Robertson Davies*

*C*anada might be a mother, but Michigan was a mistress.

— *John Kenneth Galbraith*

*W*e too often tend to apologize for drawing to someone's attention that they are standing on our feet.

— *Brian Tobin*

*Y*ou can always tell a Canadian by the fact that when he walks into a room, he automatically chooses to sit in the most uncomfortable chair.

— *Peter C. Newman*

*C*anadians do not like heroes, and so they do not have them.

— *George Woodcock*

*I*n Canada we don't ban demonstrations,
we reroute them.

— *Alan Borovoy*

*I*n this country you can say what you like
because no one will listen to you anyway.

— *Margaret Atwood*

*C*anadians love Canada,
but not for fifty-two weeks of the year.

— *Jean Chrétien*

*A*dam was a Canadian. Nobody but a Canadian
would stand in a perfect tropical garden beside a
perfectly naked woman and worry about an apple.

— *Dave Broadfoot*

*T*he genius of Canada remains essentially
a deflationary genius.

— *Jan Morris*

$\mathcal{C}$anada's national bird is the grouse.

— *Stuart Keate*

$\mathcal{C}$[$\mathcal{C}$anada is] the Woody Allen of nations.

— *John Gray*

$\mathcal{S}$tick a pin in Canadian literature at random, and nine times out of ten you'll find a victim.

— *Margaret Atwood*

*C*anadians are perversely loath
to face up to any good news.

— *John W. Holmes*

*A*s far as mental health is concerned,
Canada is still in the ox-cart days.

— *C.M. Hincks, mental health pioneer*

*W*e worry when you look hard at us,
but we are also touchy about being overlooked.

— *Lester Pearson*

*E*verybody in this country has the psychology of a minority group, and not a very important minority either.

— *Charles Hood*

*T*here's nothing to link a person from Winnipeg with someone from Quebec, unless they're in Venice together, sitting in St. Mark's Square drinking cappuccino.

— *Robert Lepage*

*C*anada has never been a melting pot,
more like a tossed salad.

— *Arnold Edinborough*

✎

*W*e are all immigrants to this place
even if we were born here.

— *Margaret Atwood*

✎

I pray in French;
I work in English part of the time
and I dream about things American.

— *Jules Léger*

$\mathcal{A}$ Canadian is someone who keeps asking the question, "What is a Canadian?"

— *Irving Layton*

"$\mathcal{C}$anadian identity" is an oxymoron.

— *Anonymous*

$\mathcal{O}$ne Canadian is an identity crisis. Two make a separatist threat.

— *Eric Korn*

*C*anada is the existence of not being.
Not English, not American.
We're more like celery as a flavour.

— *Mike Myers*

*C*anada is the only country in the world
that knows how to live without an identity.

— *Marshall McLuhan*

*C*anada is a country where everyone feels
so much more comfortable with amateurs.

— *Barbara Amiel*

*M*ost of us are still huddled tight to the border,
looking into the candy store window,
scared by the Americans on one side
and the bush on the other.

— *Mordecai Richler*

*S*ome are born great,
some achieve greatness,
some have greatness thrust upon them,
and some remained in Canada.

— *Eric Nicol*

*C*anadian culture is at the very front of the second rank.

— *Barry Callaghan*

*C*ontemplating the arts in Canada [is] like listening to Mozart while suffering from a toothache.

— *Peter M. Dwyer*

*T*he reason Canadian poetry is not considered great poetry is because the Canadian army is only a small army.

— *Milton Acorn*

*M*argaret Atwood, Margaret Laurence — never heard of them, so they must be Canadian.

— *Anonymous Canadian high school student*

*I*n Canada we may know little about literature, but we are great experts on questions of respectability.

— *Robertson Davies*

*H*ail our great Queen in her regalia
One foot in Canada, the other in Australia.

— *James Gay*

*I*f I were English, Canada
Should love me like the deuce,
But I was born in Canada
So what the hell's the use.

— *Wilson MacDonald*

*E*ngland would be better off without Canada.

— *Napoleon Bonaparte*

*C*anada is the only country in the world
where you can buy a book on federal–provincial relations
at an airport.

— *Michael Valpy*

I sometimes think a Canadian's idea of heaven
is an eternal panel discussion.

— *Marc Lalonde*

The fabric of Canadian cities leans to
architectural polyester.

— *William Thorsell*

In Canada there is a certain frankness about the
basic structure of a building.

— *John C. Parkin*

The beer parlours on the Prairies are sacred places;
they organize the landscape as the
cathedrals organize Europe.

— *Robert Kroetsch*

$\mathcal{T}$he sky over Ottawa or Toronto or Montreal
is still singularly unstained by any
transcendent work of human genius.

— *E.K. Brown*

$\mathcal{I}$ believe it will take a thousand years
to develop a national style in Canada, but
I do see a light in the west over a grain elevator.

— *Eric Arthur*

*W*hen I was [in Canada] I found their jokes like
their roads — very long and not very good, leading to a
little tin point of a spire which has been remorselessly
obvious for miles without seeming to get any nearer.

— *Samuel Butler*

*E*ven when Canadian humour is awful
it just lies there being awful in its own fresh way.

— *Robert Thomas Allen*

*C*anada's problem is that it has too much sense
and not enough humor.

— *Godfrey Just*

*C*anada is a private joke shared by all Canadians,
but we don't like other people getting in on it.

— *Sean Kelly*

*C*anada is so square that even the
female impersonators are women.

— *from the film* Outrageous

❧

*I*n Canada, when they hold a beauty contest,
they don't give the first prize to the prettiest girl,
because she already has something.

— *Lorne Michaels*

❧

*C*anadian girls are so pretty
it is a relief to see a plain one now and then.

— *Mark Twain*

*C*anadian love, Canadian love.
It's forty below or ninety above.

— *Marie-Lynn Hammond*

A Canadian is someone who knows
how to make love in a canoe.

— *Pierre Berton*

We have cunningly put our potential muggers into team sweaters, shoving them out on the ice, paying them handsomely to spear, slash and high stick or whatever.

— *Mordecai Richler*

Canadian hockey has been carried to all parts of the world, usually on a stretcher.

— *Eric Nicol and Dave Moore*

If you can't beat 'em in the alley, you can't beat 'em on the ice.

— *Conn Smythe*

*G*enerally in Canadian sports coverage, if you can't catch it,
throw it, or hit it with a stick, nobody
wants to know about it.

— *Randy Black*

*I*n English-speaking Canada, hockey sometimes
seems to be the sole assurance that we have a culture.

— *Rick Salutin*

*S*eparatism is all very fine in theory,
but what would they call the Montreal hockey team?

— Globe and Mail *editorial, 1976*

*T*here is only one class on the plains, and that is
the working class. Here and there you meet a
gentleman of leisure, but he is called a tramp.

— *Howard A. Kennedy, 1907*

*W*hen a nation's elite is three generations removed
from steerage, it cannot afford too many pretensions.

— *Peter C. Newman*

*F*or real wealth and real power in Canada,
inherit it, or marry it,
or forget it.

— *Walter Stewart*

*L*et the Old World, where rank's yet vital,
Part those who have and have not title.
Toronto has no social classes —
Only the Masseys and the masses.

— *B.K. Sandwell*

*H*ere, every man is the son of his own works.

— *Thomas D'Arcy McGee, 1865*

*W*e are over-protected under-achievers.

— *Robert Scrivener*

*T*o be poor in America means you are not trying very hard.
To be poor in Canada means that the government
is not trying hard enough.

— *Val Sears*

*R*ich by nature, poor by policy,
might be written over Canada's door.

— *Goldwin Smith*

*T*here is little passion in Canadian life.
Suspicion and jealousy of the United States and
for England are not passions.

— *A.L. Phelps*

*A*ll that Canada owes to Great Britain
is a great deal of Christian forgiveness.

— *Sir Richard Cartwright, 1888*

*I*n recent years the Canadian government has managed
to bring everything under its control except
the national debt and the budget.

— *John F. Bulloch*

*C*anada is probably the world's richest
underdeveloped country.

— *Alexander Ross*

*C*anada is not so much a country as
magnificent raw material for a country.

— *Alden Nowlan*

I'm on my way to Canada,
That cold and dreary land;
The dire effects of slavery
I can no longer stand . . .
Farewell, old master,
Don't come after me,
I'm on my way to Canada
Where colored men are free.

— *"Away to Canada" (American slave song, 1851)*

*T*hey're about the only ones
who still believe in it all,
the Canadians.

— *John Le Carré*